Believe YOUR WAY TO

BADASS

The Interactive Guide to Redefining your Beliefs,
Developing your Self-love, and Manifesting your Way to
your Best, Most Badass Self

Celeste Rains-Turk

Celeste Rains-Turk

www.celestial.fit

I dedicate this book to my amazing, supportive, and loving family. Thank you for always being encouraging and understanding of who I am, my dreams, my missions, and my choices. I appreciate you all in more ways than words could ever express. There is never a day when my heart is not full of gratitude for our family. With all the warmth of which you each accept me for exactly who I am and all of my growth, there is no way else to express my deep love for each of you. I am so happy and grateful to have a family which I can celebrate my passions with knowing that I have unconditional love and support from each of you. With all my love, I dedicate this book to you guys.

This interactive guide is built to lead you to discover, build, and unleash your inner Badass through step-by-step coaching and journaling prompts. This guide can be used for all aspects of your life which further your badassery.

CELESTE'S STORY/LETTER FROM CELESTE

Hey there!

I am really excited to be bringing this interactive guide/book to you. These are not only the tools and strategies and resources I use for myself, but for my VIP 1:1 clients and VIP membership site members as well. You may be wondering a bit about me like who I am, what have I been through, etc. SO, let's jump right in with a little summary about me.

I was born December 5, 1996. I have grown up in a loving, supportive, awesome home with two amazing parents and my older sister. We did a lot of traveling as a family growing up, which is how I think I developed my love for travel. My family is also very active: I tried ballet, gymnastics, ice skating, tennis, soccer, and indoor and beach volleyball. I was pretty chubby growing up until about middle school, and sometimes I would be teased for it, but it didn't really bring me down for too long because I was always an athlete and always very sporty. I loved soccer so much I could have sworn I would be the next Mia Hamm. Well, I wasn't because then I met Volleyball. I had to decide which one I wanted to travel for and play on a club team for. I chose volleyball and I played competitively from 11-19 years-old. My goal was to play collegiately, and I actually committed to but that all changed because of my love and passion for fitness.

In 2012, I stood in front of the mirror and I hated what I saw. I hated that I didn't feel as well as I could or thought I deserved to. I hated that I didn't look like the skilled athlete I was. I hated not being confident in my skin like I was in myself on a personality scale. I hated that I couldn't eat whatever I wanted without gaining fat like most of my friends. I hated that I had an unproportioned body with large volleyball legs and nearly no upper body. I hated that I knew I could be better but wasn't. I hated that guys kept walking all over me. I hated that I was being cheated, lied to, and deceived. I hated the way people were treating me. I hated the way I felt. I hated the jiggle. I hated the self-consciousness. I hated the towel wrapping to hide in a bikini. I hated that I couldn't wear tight tank tops or feel really good in short shorts. I hated that the outside didn't match the inside.

So, I changed. I made a decision. I started working out from home and changing the way I ate. I burned a LOT of fat. I started off pretty weak and felt myself get stronger every day. I went from barely being able to do 5 leg lifts to knocking out 20 with ease, among other remarkable changes with endurance and energy. After some time, I started treating myself like a guinea pig. I was trying different things, I was eating differently, I was mixing it up, I was just doing all sorts of different things. I even took up (and still train) Ju-Jitsu.

After a year or so, I decided I wanted to step it up. I needed a gym membership, but it was my responsibility to pay for it. I could have easily said, "I don't have the money" and made excuses, but I believe if you want something bad enough you make it happen. So, I got a job as a volleyball coach, and the money I earned went straight into a gym membership. You could think of this as my first investment, moneywise, in myself—And you better believe my self-worth went up with it. Then I really wanted to step it up. I always saw myself as this fit, healthy, strong, muscular, defined female, and since I wasn't there I made another decision. I hired an online trainer for a couple of weeks, some of you may recognize the name, Paige Hathaway. She helped me to achieve a much better look but something was still missing.

Throughout High School I was very depressed and suicidal. Even though I was also EXTREMELY happy, outgoing, fun, successful, and level-headed, I still suffered. I absolutely loved my life, so I could not quite wrap my head around this. When I attempted suicide, I had a huge realization that I needed help and would never do that again. Then time passed, I didn't get the help I needed, and my junior or senior year rolled around and I had deep depression again. So badly that my friends actually reported me to the school. That was actually one of the turning points for me. I finally got the help I needed. It took maybe 10 therapy sessions to actually feel better about everything and to gain clarity. In all honesty though, I believe my depression was a choice I made. I chose to have it, I chose to fuel it, I chose to focus on it. I focused on it so much before I got help and somewhat during that I actually created another mental illness. I then found myself facing anxiety. I literally created this because I was focusing on depression to the point where I was so fearful of myself. I share this story and many other personal stories on my Facebook, so please feel free to connect with me there.

www.celestial.fit

When I found fitness, it helped a lot of those struggles, but it didn't solve everything. Like I said, I was achieving my goals but I knew something was still missing. By this time I already decided I no longer wanted to be an interior designer which was my original plan, and I decided I 100% wanted to pursue fitness. So, I started job shadowing trainers, reading, learning, getting educated, getting certified and then, started this business. Currently, I am a certified personal trainer through the National Academy of Sports Medicine (NASM) and a student of Dietetics at Kansas State University (Global Campus-Online).

When I started my business, I was graduated from high school because I graduated early. I knew I wanted to be an online trainer and help people all over the world. I wasn't as clear on my mission and my message as I am now. Back then I just knew I wanted to give people what fitness gave me. But after some time. I did a LOT of soul searching.

I had committed to play volleyball collegiately; I was all set to go and everything. But in my last year of club volleyball, I practically cried every time I stepped on the court. I was crying because I was grieving. I still loved it and loved everything it had given me but it wasn't for me anymore. In my heart I knew this. In my heart I didn't want to go play college ball. I wanted to move on. I wanted to fully commit to my business and my life in fitness. I had to let go of the old Celeste, the young girl who always wanted to play in college, the last 8 years of my life spent developing as a player to play in college. I had to let all of that go. It was not hard to know the answer, because we always know what is right or wrong. We know how things should feel. I knew, it was the announcing, and the grieving that was difficult. I sometimes questioned myself but I always had an answer, I always knew what I really wanted. I followed that. I was no longer "the volleyball girl" I became "the fitness girl" "the lifter" "the gym rat" "the business owner" "the passionate power woman" "the trainer" and, most importantly, I fully stepped into my role as "Celeste."

I was always trying to figure out what it was that was missing when I was starting my own journey. I was thinking of other coaches I had, or programs I did, or nutrition guidance I followed. Then it hit me, and it hit me HARD. I realized that my message was all about the inner growth which aids us in our journey. That was what was always missing for me in other programs. Even though my body was looking better I still wanted more confidence, happiness, love for myself, wellbeing, and inner strength and development and I realized I took myself through that and then that is what I was giving to clients. It's the mindset, the self-love, the behavior changes, the wellness dimensions and development, the inner work—THAT'S WHAT MAKES THE DIFFERENCE!

That's when Building More than Just a Body was born. My purpose, my passion, my mission, my heart, and my soul in 6 words. And damn did that and does that feel amazing. Having this clarity, having this knowing, having this awareness and realization and breakthrough allowed me to expand, grow, learn, and develop as well as share it with my clients by focusing on emphasizing the importance of self-love, self-confidence and self-esteem building strategies coming together with mindset, wellness, personal development, inner work, behavior change modification planning, and of course a proper training and nutrition regimen.

www.celestial.fit

FOREWORDS

Celeste Rains-Turk! I am so incredibly proud of you! It truly is such an honour to have been a part of your journey and see you grow and develop into the powerful leader that you are today.

I admire your work ethic, your strength, and your unique ability to create rapid and lasting change in others.

Your drive, your passion for life and your energy is not only impressive, but it is addictive when people are in your presence!

Thank you for how you show up in this world and thank you for being committed to having such a big vision.

The world really does need more people to walk, talk, think, and act like you.

I have really enjoyed diving deep into *Believe Your Way To Badass* and particularly enjoyed the fun and conversational style that it is written in.

I feel that this book completely showcases your personality and the essence of who you are, and I know that the reader will also directly feel how much you care about them, which is truly special.

I'm really excited to see the ripple effect that this book creates in the world, as more and more people step up and manifest the most badass version of themselves!

Keep turning on lights all over the world Celeste.

You have already achieved and created so much, but I know that you are just getting started as there are so many more lives to impact.

I will continue to follow your every move in the future, because it really is people like you who are turning the world into a better place."

All my love,

Regan Hillyer
www.reganhillyer.com
Serial entrepreneur, #1 best-selling author, international speaker.

Believe your way to Badass is the catalyst that you need to allow yourself to live your dream life.

This book is so profound in its principles that I've read it twice just to ingrain its powerful concepts into my mind.

Celeste has made some major shifts in her life and it is by these exact strategies that you will make profound shifts in your life as well.

www.celestial.fit

I have known Celeste for quite some time, as I am her business coach. She came to me at the young age of 18 wanting to create a global online business that helps others.

I was so fascinated by the passion, drive, and conviction this young woman had that I took her on as a student. Since then, she has blown my mind with how much passion she has.

I'm so glad that she decided to write this book. I am even more honored that she chose me to write this foreword.

Celeste is a powerful woman who changes many lives and an icon in this world. This book will be one of many that she writes and I know that it will change your life.

I've read many books in my day, but this one will transform your life! It seriously gets my highest recommendation.

With Love,

AJ Mihrzad

Author of the *MIND BODY Solution: Train Your Brain for Permanent Weight Loss*

Founder of OnlineSupercoach.com

INSPIRATION FOR CREATION

I have created this interactive guide/journal because I truly want you to receive the maximum benefits, enjoy the experience, and be empowered to fully step into your badass self. I find the best way to achieve anything in life is by actually taking action. After all it is pretty hard to have something if we don't go out and get it. My whole life I have always loved the word badass. I understand it means different things for different people and we will get into all of that VERY soon.

As mentioned above, I am a huge advocate for all things self-love and confidence. My message and my mission is to help others build more than just a body. This means that I not only coach people to their best aesthetic body but also to their most clear, strong, aligned mind and wellbeing. Self-love is a huge deal on any journey—like say, LIFE! I want to give you the ability to allow yourself to commit to you, your development, and what you want.

Self-Love is not just about affirmations and self-talk. Like most things in life, action speaks louder than words. This guide is going to be an epic way for you to show yourself love. While you will develop daily rituals from this to your liking it is important to note that every time you pick up this guide and go through the prompts you are showing yourself love.

It is important that you go at your own pace and one that empowers you to be consistent and excited. I recommend spending time on these. Give them some thought. Not because you need to, but because you deserve this. This is all for you! Even if it may not seem easy to accept or embrace that fully, by the end of this guide it will be so much easier.

Cool thing is, you can do this OVER and OVER and OVER again. Because, last time I checked, we never stop growing and there are always ways to improve.

Let's do this! ☺

WHAT TO EXPECT

In this guide I am going to be giving you some of my BEST strategies. We are going to dive DEEP together. I will guide you through each prompt and share information around each and what it all means. It is important to read everything as one word could switch it all on for you and I don't want you to miss out on anything. If you find yourself starting to feel like "I will do this later" or "I will do this part tomorrow" or "I don't really want to write today or anymore" then SLOW down. We don't want to self-sabotage through overwhelm. So breathe, trust, and relax. This is not a race, this is not a competition, this is you diving deep into yourself—don't stress it, just take action, and choose to place positive energy around each and every word, prompt, action, and feeling that comes up for you.

Some of this may be seemingly challenging, some of this may be seemingly easy, some of this may be scary, some of this may be fun (all of it let's be honest). Key thing is to keep on going, because that's what badasses do right? YES! When you see a ☐ , just put a little check mark or x in there, if it feels fitting for you ☺

I am going to be doing a lot of conversational type writing—that's just how I write. So if it feels like I am sitting next to you or walking you through this, GOOD! I may ask questions, some may be serious, some may be rhetorical, either way the answers are ALWAYS within YOU, remember that. THE ANSWERS ALWAYS COME FROM WITHIN! Can you commit to that? Check ☐ yes or ☐ yes. ☺ COOL!

Okay so I also want to provide a bit of a disclaimer, I am a little quirky, I am a lot of fun, and I am totally genuinely myself. So if you wonder why some things may get goofy, funny, or playful, well because, that's how I want to run this show. I believe life has to be driven from within. And honestly, our outside world is a reflection of our inner world, so considering I love weird, unusual, authentic, unique things and people and experiences, I am, of course, finding that within.

I would ask you for permission to be myself but then again, why should I? Not only would that go against everything I am about and this is about but it would be a disservice to you. By being myself I am able to empower you to do the same. I have given myself that permission, if you don't like that then, I encourage you firstly to give yourself permission to be 100% yourself and then watch as the beauty of authenticity shines from all of us and those around you. I am committed to creating a space for others to always feel comfortable with being open, honest, and 100% themselves. Even If this doesn't apply to you and you are already there that is awesome and I am so happy to be creating this space for you to dig deeper, show the world more of you, and embrace your badass self.

www.celestial.fit

Everyone has a gift, what is yours? Don't dim the light, ever! One of my friends shared a quote with me along the lines of choosing to be like the stars or the sun and the best thing about the sun is it doesn't give a f%*$ if it blinds you; so let that badass shine so bright from within you that you aren't afraid to blind the world with it. Seriously, the world NEEDS it, it NEEDS you. Let's just ALL commit to being ourselves shall we?

There will be space for you to journal in the guide, however you can also have your own journal for this, it is all up to you how you would like to go about this. If you don't want to use this journal space provided or think you will need more, then I recommend just using your own journal. Some people like to type on a computer or on their phone, others like to write. Just do what will personally benefit you the most! ☺

Some Words I Find Myself Using When I Think of or Describe the Book:

- Empower
- Unleash
- Grow
- Develop
- Discover
- Release
- Accept
- Love
- Believe
- Know

- Learn
- Trust
- Identity
- Action
- Alignment
- Uplevel
- Choice
- Decision
- And, of course, Badass

LET'S DOUBLE CHECK THAT *THIS* IS FOR *YOU*

(Likelihood is it is, if you have made it this far)

Place a checkmark in each box which describes you

☐ You want to Believe your way to Badass

☐ You want to learn more about and do more self-development

☐ You are open to mindset work

☐ You are willing to put in the work

☐ You are ready to feel empowered (or more empowered)

☐ You want to grow

☐ You want to develop

☐ You want to release old/new/any limiting beliefs

☐ You want to have more self-love, self-confidence, and self-esteem

☐ You want to step into the power of you

☐ You are open minded and ready to allow yourself to fully immerse yourself in this process with me

www.celestial.fit

CONTENTS

OPERATION BADASS: CLARITY

It is really important to first gain some clarity on everything in order to gain the absolute most from this experience. The main reason I want it to be interactive is because it is a great thing to read, or be taught but we don't really learn or benefit until we apply. I made a commitment to myself and in my business that I would always serve others. I felt called to make this book interactive for that reason. Granted, you can choose to benefit, apply, and interact with any book, anytime! However, I really want to see you dive deep with all of this.

What is clarity anyways? Other than a word that gets used a lot, clarity is essential in all things. Without it, well, things would be unclear. Imagine you have some glasses on right now, or just anytime in life. Usually what happens is we wear glasses which can be a bit, well, foggy. Sometimes we have our judgmental glasses on, somedays we have our gratitude glasses, and sometimes we have our inquisitive glasses on.

A lot of times we wear judgement to protect ourselves. Maybe there's been a time where something or someone has not treated you as you would hope, expect, or like, or maybe it didn't all turn out as planned and then we create a specific judgement. What then happens is someone or something or some event could trigger that. We walk around with these glasses to catch those types of triggers, it's a guard which doesn't serve us though. Just because it happened in the past, doesn't mean it is bound to happen again, unless you are burned from playing with fire, but that's just logic.

Now let's consider wearing our gratitude glasses. This means we are in a state of appreciation, adoration, or even acceptance. You are just taking it all in. It's one of those days where the sun shines extra bright, or the rain doesn't bother you, or your bed is extra comfy, or you hug a little longer, and stare a little deeper, and share a little more. These are one of the coolest glasses you own, seriously, these are the ones we should wear more often but sometimes leave in the car.

Okay, now let's look at our inquisitive pair. Oooh, these are kind of cool. I wonder where they were made? Where were they bought? Are all the parts from the same place? I wonder who made the signature on the side? Why did they choose this color? I am so curious. I just want to know more. Tell me more, more, more. These glasses are going to be really important for when you are asking yourself questions. These are the ones you wear when you are on a date, or you are interviewing someone, or you are people watching, or you are watching TV or reading a mystery novel or wondering what someone is thinking, or how you can help someone. These are one of my favorite pairs to wear, along with appreciation of course.

Why am I pinning these types of approaches as glasses? Because it is easy to just grab a pair and put them on without thinking about it. It is important to be aware of what glasses we are wearing. It is also important to put particular ones on in different situations and different circumstances. Throughout this book let's agree to put the judgmental glasses down and keep our inquisitive and gratitude glasses readily available.

Basically, I don't want you to judge yourself, feel judged, or lose touch with your deepest self because of the little subconscious voice in your head judging you or telling you stories that aren't true (ex: you aren't worthy, you aren't capable, you don't deserve this). I also want you to know that I have put my judgement glasses away too, this is a judgement free zone. Let's be curious about ourselves, and show ourselves some love and appreciation. This is going to be a deep interaction with yourself, and I want to encourage lots of positive, loving, expansive, experiences within you. If you find yourself feeling strange, or negative, or mean, check what glasses you are wearing; usually the judgement glasses are the ones that feel the worst. You may find yourself struggling to show yourself love, don't worry, you are doing it right, you may just need some time for yourself to get used to the appreciation and love that it so deeply deserves.

OPERATION BADASS: CLARITY

PART 1: SETTING INTENTIONS

To get started, I want you to spend some time on setting intentions. You may be thinking, "What the hell is an 'intention'?" Well, intentions, among other tools I will share with you, have accelerated my growth because they provide meaning to action. SO, to set an intention, it is important to ask yourself questions like this:

> "What do I want to get out of reading and taking part in this book?" (How do you want it to change your life?)

> "Why do I believe this book will help me?"

> "At the end of this, I want to... feel x or be more y or act more z..."

The reason I want you to set intentions, and the reason why intentions are so important is because they are preparing you, your current identity, and your mind for success. What you focus on you find, so when we can be clear on what we actually want out of doing something we are more likely to achieve it, agree? ☐

Imagine if we set intentions for everything? How huge would that be? What type of a difference would that make? To be so clear on what it is you ACTUALLY want to achieve, or gain, or learn, or feel is a powerful thing to tap into everyday! Without intentions we would basically be going in without any end goal in mind (don't worry we are getting into goals VERY SOON and this will be helpful to refer back to). Intentions allow us to open our mind to a bigger picture, they allow us to choose what we want, they allow us to decide what we are going to get, and intentions allow us to dictate the level of which we commit to playing at, showing up at, or succeeding at. Are there rules? NO! Should there be? NO! Do you want there to be? You decide.

Allow yourself to feel free, in control, and empowered to choose your outcomes, your life, your success, who you are, what you do, how you feel, who you spend time with, and literally any aspect of life because, key word here is, YOUR life ;) Write it from a place of it being done...ex: I am so happy and grateful that I feel x, y, z...

Set Intentions Here:

_____
_____
_____
_____
_____
_____
_____
_____
_____
_____
_____
_____
_____
_____
_____
_____
_____
_____

_____

_____

_____

_____

_____

_____

_____

_____

_____

_____

_____

_____

_____

_____

_____

_____

_____

_____

_____

_____

_____

_____

_____

_____

_____

OPERATION BADASS: CLARITY

PART 2: DEFINING BADASS

Now it's time to define badass, what does it mean to you? The beauty is you get to define and choose and dictate everything in your life. Honestly, everything goes through your unique filtering system anyways, so you are always defining and choosing but sometimes that can be overridden by thinking about what we have been told, learned, or what others would say about it all.

So, in this part of the book I want you to only listen to your own voice. When I say badass, what is the FIRST thing you think of? Let go of anything you have been told before about 'being a badass', let go of anything that has held you back from deciding that you are your own badass, and just choose, today, right now; What does badass mean to you?

Defining this is going to set the stage for the rest of the exercises (don't worry your definition may change as you grow, this is not set in stone, definitive, or a one-time only deal). The reason for defining is so we can have a clear idea of what our end goal or ideal reality or most desired outcome actually looks like. It's not about how yours stacks up to others, it's just about you, and your interpretation of the word, badass. We cannot hit a target that we cannot see, so make sure you can see it by first defining it. The rest will appear throughout this experience.

BADASS/ 'bad,as/ North American—informal; can be used as an adjective or a noun;

YOUR DEFINITION:

_____

_____

_____

_____

_____

_____

_____

_____

_____

_____

_____

_____

_____

_____

_____

_____

_____

_____

_____

_____

_____

_____

_____

_____

_____

_____

_____

_____

_____

_____

_____

_____

_____

_____

_____

_____

_____

_____

_____

_____

_____

_____

_____

_____

OPERATION BADASS: CLARITY

PART 3: WHO ARE YOU RIGHT NOW?

So now that you have clarity on what being a badass means to you, let's look at where you are at right now. Any transformation begins somewhere. This is the beginning of your journey. You get to decide what the journey is going to be. Who are you right now is about being aware of your present in order to prepare for your future. Like most transformations we always start with an initial measurement; this is your measurement. I want you to be detailed with this one. Most people don't take the time to actually define themselves. It is easy for us to define other things in our life or some sort of ideal or perfect picture, but who we are right now matters more than anything, because well you matter the most in your life as you are the catalyst for everything.

Given that you are the catalyst for every part of your life, I want you to consider a few things: How do you look? How do you act? How do you eat? How do you spend your free time? What do you think about when you day dream? How much sleep are you getting-does it matter to you? How do you feel on average? Do you take responsibility for your life-How much? Are you seeking solutions? Do you invest in yourself? How do you speak to yourself? Where do you spend the most time? How committed are you to yourself? Are you working? Do you love what you do? How do you feel when you look in the mirror? Who are you surrounded by? Are the people and things (environment around you) serving you? And keep asking questions like this. DIG DEEP!!

Do this from a space of genuine, authentic, real, honesty. Allow yourself to recognize aspects of your life; no judgement just evaluation. Don't even consider how you stack up against the badass definition, this is about YOU, right now. Applaud yourself for taking part in this exercise and getting in touch with yourself. Your mind and soul will thank you for paying attention. Some of this may be difficult to admit, you may realize some things, you may find yourself doubting yourself, questioning, or thinking you have to solve everything all at once, or maybe you feel like your life is pretty perfect as is and you don't need improving—keeping in mind a form of self-sabotage can be thinking you have no problems, and nothing to improve.

Also, this is not meant to be all negatives. This is all honesty with yourself. For example, when I do this I highlight that I have a very high standard of health, wellbeing, fitness, mindset, and confidence. I highlight that I love what I do and I always 100% myself. When we can be honest about all aspects of our life, shit can shift faster.

You can bullet, write out, rate, draw, color code, anything YOU need to do to have a clear understanding of who you are right now! (by the way, I would definitely highlight the fact that you are taking the time to have this experience of Believe your way to Badass) that is a HUGE win! (See the next 2 pages for journaling space—I did two because, if you are like me, you could write all day. Of course, use the backs, too!)

Who am I right now?!

_____

_____

_____

_____

_____

_____

_____

_____

_____

_____

_____

_____

_____

_____

_____

OPERATION BADASS: APPRECIATION

I have to be honest, this is one of, if not my most favorite part of any journey. The importance of showing oneself appreciation and love and support is unmatched by anything I know. While we can love and be loved deeply by others, it is so much easier to receive love when we not only give it to others but first ourselves. Something I would put on a NYC Times Square Bill Board would be something I always say to myself and clients when applicable, "Love yourself, the more love you have inside, then the more love you can radiate to others and ultimately the more love you can receive"

This was a huge turning point in my journey. My message is all about Building More than Just a Body and this is where it all began. I realized the fitness and health industry was growing yet everyone was still 'feeling stuck' or 'unhappy with their body' or 'couldn't achieve their goals'. Obesity, on the rise, mental illness, on the rise, eating disorders, yep you guessed it, on the rise. There is no doubt in my mind the reason the industry grows yet others do not is because the area which requires the most growth is being neglected, big time.

The moment I realized that was the same moment I chose to give more to myself. My journey changed. I no longer just saw results on the outside, but I felt results. I finally got what I was searching for the whole time which was inner strength. My journey didn't start by me going, "WOW, I really want to have the hottest body in all the land" (although that is okay if that is your goal ☺). I personally started from a place of hating that my aesthetic body did not represent the beauty of which I knew I had within. It started when I didn't have the confidence in myself or the self-esteem I desired. My journey required self-love, and inner work, so, I gave myself that.

Love and appreciation can be shown in so many different ways. It is important to find which ways work best for you. I know they all work for me and I love to use them all. Speaking to yourself in a loving tone or from a positive space, expression through actions like eating a nutritious meal or working out or getting a massage, buying yourself a gift-maybe flowers, pampering yourself, listening to your body, and trusting your instinct. Sometimes what happens is we feel like we aren't allowed to do these things; that they are selfish, or don't benefit others around us, or take from our loved ones, or limit us, or take time, or are uncomfortable, or weird, or make us narcissist. However, being 'selfish' is one of the most 'selfless' things you can do. When we show ourselves love and appreciation and understanding we are able to maximize on those feelings and consistently deliver that energy to everyone around us. We raise the vibrations and the state of those in our environment. We are able to receive more from others because we allow ourselves to generate it from within. Remember, we radiate and receive.

When we take care of ourselves, there is no doubt we perform better for everyone around us, or in our work, or our hobbies, or our time in general.

When we give permission to ourselves to let go and accept this warmth from within it makes for an easier time giving it to the world, and then allows us to be conditioned to accepting it, so we easily accept from others, which is appreciated by all. It is difficult to serve anyone if we don't even serve ourselves. You know the old analogy of putting your gas mask on first before helping others? Yeah, that's so you don't DIE. If you die, you can't help anyone else. So, if you want to give more love to others, give to yourself. The most important piece I want to leave you with knowing before beginning this portion of the book is that if you desire more love, warmth, or positivity from others, or you aren't getting any, or you are uncomfortable with receiving it (i.e, a compliment), look within first. Give yourself that FIRST because your outer world is a direct reflection of your inner world so commit to yourself.

OPERATION BADASS: APPRECIATION

PART 1: SELF-LOVE VS. SELF LOATHE

The concept came to me one day after hearing, seeing, and reading so many people talking to or about or what they are doing from a place of loathe. I realized we have so many options to speak from a place of love, gratitude, warmth, appreciation, positivity, etc. Yet so often we choose doubt, shame, sadness, limiting beliefs, hatred, disgust, and restriction. Let me tell you, from personal experience, and from witnessing others in a place of self –loathe, it really doesn't get you anywhere but down.

Self-loathe doesn't feel great. It feels a bit harsh, a bit wild, a bit unsettling. We know when we are loathing because it doesn't sit well with us. We recognize it and then we justify it. We are mean and hateful and sometimes we don't know it because it is so engrained in us, it is part of the language of people surrounding us, it is so common to your mind, your soul doesn't know much other treatment. I was in such a state of self-loathe that all I did was attract more of it, again what you focus on you find. Because I was speaking to myself hatefully and I was creating this inner toxicity I began calling in people who did the same to me; walked all over, cheated on, lied to, verbal abuse, and more. This was my responsibility. I created an inner world so toxic the outer world could only mirror that which I created within.

My soul craved the love. Don't get me wrong, I have and had a lot of love, support, and excitement in my life. I had moments where I felt on top of the world, no doubt. But I wanted more of it and I knew I deserved more of it. So, I committed to having more of it. And now, it is your turn.

When I began using this powerful tool I began attracting more love, support, appreciation, and non-toxic relationships and experiences into my life. It is never too late to turn things around for yourself. When we can turn within and generate positive change in our own life, we allow those around us to do the same. Be the catalyst.

Let's compare the two using real-life examples, then you will fill in the diagram with examples of your own. Begin with ways you have spoken to yourself in loathe, then re-write the same things in love. This exercise may be challenging but allow the examples provided to get the wheels turning. Oh, and don't be so hard on yourself for any times where you have loathed instead of love, instead just recognize the beauty of this moment where you are taking the time to acknowledge a language which no longer serves you and you are finally giving yourself what you deserve. *inhale the great*

Self-Loathe Says

Self-Loathe Language:

"I can't eat that cookie because it will all go to my stomach fat and love handles"

"I have to go to the gym today because if I don't I will always be this ugly, gross human being..."

"I hate my body"

"I can't go because I have really low self-esteem and I don't even look good in a bikini/board-shorts"

"I will never be able to x I am too y"

Self-Love Statements/New Language

"I eat nutritious meals because it makes my body feel so amazing, refreshed, and ready to fuel my awesome workout"

"I go to the gym because it reminds me of all the positive steps I am taking to show myself more love, respect, and care. The gym makes my body feel stronger, healthier, and makes me feel more confident and happy, I can't wait to go workout!"

"I love my body for all that it gives me and its ability to grow, transform, and improve. My body deserves love."

"I am excited to go and connect with these amazing people. I don't have to wear a bikini to feel good about myself and I know if I did I would rock it anyways because I commit to owning my body and I know I am giving it the attention it deserves to feel strong inside and out by focusing on Building More than just a Body."

"I am capable of anything and everything I set my mind too and I always make things happen or work."

Self-Love Says

www.celestial.fit

Begin with ways you have spoken to yourself in loathe,
  then re-write them in love.

_____

_____

_____

_____

_____

_____

_____

_____

_____

_____

_____

_____

_____

_____

_____

_____

_____

_____

_____

_____

OPERATION BADASS: APPRECIATION

PART 2: WHERE IS THE LOVE?

THIS! This is going to be HUGE. I teach this in even more depth to my members and clients, however I want to bring this to you, too. The importance of showing ourselves love is, like I mentioned, unmatched. This next exercise has potential to feel uncomfortable, strange, and a little 'self-indulgent'. I know that when I express love for myself I feel so great, and sometimes when I express love for myself in front of others it gets shunned or shied away from; this is why it is so important to me.

When anything comes up around doing this, I want you to consider these feelings, where are they really coming from, are they actually your beliefs or did they come from someone or somewhere else? Naturally I believe we are meant to love ourselves to survive. However, I think beliefs have been skewed or poured into our heads that this is wrong and not at all something we should do daily let alone all day. I really believe it is time things change in the world, and what better way than for us to look within so it can then find its way out, let's start recognizing our love right now.

www.celestial.fit

Depth doesn't matter, just recognize your greatness right now...

So, what do you love about yourself, badass? ☺

_____

_____

_____

_____

_____

_____

_____

_____

_____

_____

_____

_____

_____

_____

_____

_____

_____

_____

_____

_____

_____

OPERATION BADASS: APPRECIATION

PART 3: SHOW ME THE LOVE

AWESOME! Now that we know you love at least ONE thing about yourself, let's expand on that. Have you always recognized the things you love about yourself? Something really important is to actually express the love you have for yourself. I know it can be difficult to even get in touch with what you love about yourself, but I believe that is an exercise you should be doing daily. However, words only go so far. Let's amplify the feeling we just generated from recognition and turn it into action.

Since we love ourselves, why wouldn't we maximize this love?

I want you to consider ways you show yourself love. Remember, love can be expressed in many forms. How do you speak to yourself? How do you treat yourself? How do you take care of your mind? How much attention do you give yourself? How much time do you spend on yourself? Do you set aside 'me' time? Who are you surrounding yourself with? Are you giving yourself what you want and deserve? Are you investing time, effort, and money in yourself? How often?

Think about ways you currently show yourself love (yes, taking time to read this book and make it an experience for yourself is a way):

_____

_____

_____

_____

_____

_____

_____

_____

_____

_____

_____

_____

_____

_____

_____

_____

_____

_____

_____

_____

_____
_____
_____
_____
_____
_____
_____
_____
_____
_____
_____
_____
_____
_____
_____
_____
_____
_____
_____
_____
_____
_____
_____
_____
_____
_____

OPERATION BADASS: APPRECIATION

PART 4: UP-LEVELING YOUR LOVE

Now it is time to grow. So, we have a few options:

A. Keep doing what we are doing and expect a different result

B. Do something better and get a better result.

The reason why you are heading into a search for more is because, you deserve more and you know it. You would not have chosen this book if you didn't know you deserved more. Something within you was shaking you to let yourself know, now IS the time.

So, why up-level? It is really key that we take action to enhance, improve, or step up the way we show ourselves love. This can be anything from having more or starting positive affirmations to taking yourself to get a massage every week, to eating healthier and working out, to investing in yourself or your business or what you have always dreamed of. The possibilities are endless. I love when they are endless.

* They always are *

www.celestial.fit

I want you to consider all the ways you can take your self-love to the next level. Jot down 30 or more ways you can do that and then circle, star, or somehow mark at least 5 that you commit to doing this week or this month (whatever feels best) and then start today! Repeat this exercise until it becomes habit and you don't have to think about expressing love to yourself, you just DO.

Ways I can show myself more love:

_____

_____

_____

_____

_____

_____

_____

_____

_____

_____

_____

_____

_____

_____

_____

_____

_____

_____

OPERATION BADASS: UNLOCKING YOUR POTENTIAL

All right, let's get down to business. We know you have your own definition of badass, we know you have intentions for all of this, we know you have some amount of love for yourself and a plan to up-level it, we know you are looking forward to owning your badassery, so...let's own it.

Unlocking your potential is all about finally releasing this inner badass or discovering it. Let's be honest, you know you have the ability to step into your badass best self, so it's time we figure out what that looks like. This section is going to be all about getting more clarity on what your badass definition looks like on you.

Essentially, we are going to awaken the badass by BECOMING the badass, yep, you got this. Unlocking your potential is about recognizing you have it, knowing who you must become in order to release it, and then fully stepping into that identity. No, this doesn't mean you are changing your whole life and persona (unless you really need and want to). This doesn't mean you have to become someone else, remember, you get to choose your life, who you are, and how you live. Have fun and freedom with this and know that you have so many opportunities to decide to be in your badass, but it is ultimately up to you to condition yourself to do so.

Considering you get to choose and you have full control, this is your time to really accept and give yourself permission to dig deep and understand that you have all the answers within you for this. No one can tell you what being a badass looks like, other than you. Your view on the world, your truths, are always going to be different than others, so now is your chance to rewrite or amplify your identity.

Sometimes, when people do this, they start hearing that little sucker in their head telling them things like:

1. "You don't deserve this"
2. "You could never do that"
3. "When is that even going to work for you?"
4. "You know that isn't something you have ever done so you can't now"
5. "This hasn't worked before so don't do that again because it won't work"
6. "What are you thinking, there's no way that is possible"

And that is when you then say to that little voice, I respect you, I hear you, but you no longer serve me, and for that reason I am choosing to give myself what I want and deserve and I am giving myself full permission to own who I want to be and live my life this way, thanks anyways, you can sit down now. *shoot a badass smile their way so they feel that energy ;)*

Essentially, this is your time to let loose, nothing holding you back, WHO would you BE if this was your truth? Once we answer this we can then consider what beliefs you have around becoming that person. This is where the things the voice said come in handy, remember, that voice has been conditioned into you, it has been placed and lined and woven into your subconscious and most of the time it is trying to protect you from leaving your comfort zone, but we all know growth happens outside the comfort zone. We will go deeper into the beliefs around becoming who you need to become in order to have the badass identity you deserve and desire.

Did you forget something? Well in case you did, friendly reminder that you ARE allowed to want to change, grow, and develop through working on yourself, give yourself permission now, it is time to step up and unlock your potential— ALL IN NOW.

OPERATION BADASS: UNLOCKING YOUR POTENTIAL

PART 1: CREATE A NEW...

This is going to make 100% of the difference. This is a question and an exercise you can pursue every day to achieve any goal. This is the secret sauce...and yes it tastes so good...

Essentially, we are going to take the next section as an opportunity to really come to a conclusion on who we have to become in order to be who we want to be. Believe it or not, waiting for the right time, for the right moment, for the right circumstances, does NOT propel you any closer or any faster to your ideal results. However, when we focus on becoming who we want to become and we step into that identity 'before' we have achieved the results, the results show up because that is all there is room for. If we keep around parts of our identity which don't serve us then we will keep finding reasons and ways to not have what we want or achieve our goals.

When considering becoming a badass, I want you to think about what this badass version of you does in the morning, in the day, at night, what do you eat, what do you participate in, who do you hang out with, what music do you listen to, are you seeing family and friends, are you wearing clothing-what type, what feeling fills you most of the day, how do you carry yourself-are you standing up straight or slouching or maybe you always have a hand on your head and the other on your belly, YOU DECIDE. Now is your opportunity to see yourself in that ideal reality, living life as your definition of badass. No limits, just truths. What is the badass version of YOU doing daily, seeing, feeling, etc.?

Here's the thing, if we create a space for both the results and the sabotage, we will sabotage more likely than not. An example of this would be someone who KNOWS they want to drop a pant size and it is healthy to do so, and they are saying they are committed. So they donate all their pants and go to the store and buy a pair they want to try on once they feel they have lost this last size. That person most likely will, because they have no other option, all their pants are gone so they better get to it. Now, they could have easily gotten rid of half or even none and said yeah I will get there eventually, and just stayed comfortable by not pushing out of their current reality or safety net. Main difference? One commits, the other leaves options open and knows they have a back-up plan.

How about this? NO more back up plan, no more "when this" or "when that". It is now, or never. It is 'this is it, this is my time'. When we create a space for our results to show up, they do. When we create a space for sabotage to show up, it will. Whatever we put the most focus on or energy in, expands. So, if in life, you want to lose more fat or gain more muscle and all you do is focus on it not happening, it is going to continue to not happen. Similarly, when one focuses on burning fat and gaining muscle and how it is happening and it is all

www.celestial.fit

happening right now and they decide that is the only outcome, it becomes the only outcome.

In reality, if you want to be someone different, you can't keep doing the same thing as you did the day before, you will keep getting the same results and you will not become this person who you want to be or hoped to become. This exercise allows you to depict what this ideal version of you is like to an exact tee. When we can get clear on this, visualize it, and see it, then we are able to step into it much easier. It's a matter of being the person 'before we are the person'. This creates an identity for us, a focus, and a space to generate our results. This identity will then make more conscious decisions throughout the day when the energy of this ideal person and version of us is tapped into. You will find the following page with questions to ask very helpful.

When you perform this exercise please consider questions like the ones listed on the previous page as well as the following, major thought provoker— Yes, you can ask yourself this daily!

Who do I have to become in order to achieve my results?

(BE SPECIFIC! See yourself, feel yourself, hear yourself, and understand yourself in this energetic space so you can revisit this energy over and over and over again to become this person and propel yourself forward)

_____

_____

_____

_____

_____

_____

_____

_____

_____

_____

_____

_____

_____

_____

_____

_____

OPERATION BADASS: UNLOCKING YOUR POTENTIAL

PART 2: WHAT DO YOU BELIEVE?

This is going to be huge in breaking through any limiting beliefs, self-doubt, fear, and anything else coming up for you around fully stepping into this badass version of yourself. I am really excited about sharing this high-level coaching with you and I want you to really dive deep when you ask yourself this question; "What do I believe about becoming this more badass version of myself?"

Once you ask yourself that question, consider all the ways you perceive change. Do you believe it is fast? Do you believe it is slow? Do you believe you are capable, worthy, deserving? Do you believe change is inevitable? Do you believe change is inspired? Consider what you believe about becoming this badass. Is it easy? Is it difficult? Do you believe struggle is involved in success? Do you believe you must go through hardships? Do you believe you must face difficulty? What do you REALLY believe?

What happens is beliefs get woven into our subconscious. It is important to acknowledge that they are there and again, say, you no longer serve me I am going to go this way now. We live in a world full of people with their own unique style, beliefs, truths, and outlook on the world. It is critical that we recognize if we are truly living life in our beliefs or if we have been influenced or conditioned subconsciously by others.

Sometimes, we are raised to believe success is hard work, or it takes time, or it doesn't happen to everyone, or no one can be successful doing x, y, or z. But do YOU really believe that? Do you REALLY, SERIOUSLY, and FULL HEARTEDYLY want to believe that? Pay attention to how it makes you feel to hear limiting beliefs and words such as "it's hard" or "it takes time, most people never achieve it". I struggled with similar patterns of old beliefs that I had developed in my subconscious. When I recognized them and CHOSE to believe differently, shit started to shift.

For this exercise I want you to consider all the past beliefs or even current beliefs that don't serve you and write them down. Acknowledge where they came from and why they are there. Most of the time they are there to 'protect' you, however, as discussed, they are only holding you back from achieving greatness and getting outside your zone of comfort. Once you have acknowledged them and you recognize where they come from then think about how they have served you in the past and also how they have not served you in your life and how continuing to believe in them will affect you in the long term. After you have completed all of that I then want you to make a different choice; choose to believe differently.

Ex: I choose to believe stepping into this badass version of myself will be easy and effortless because she is right there and has been ready to be unleashed for so long, now it is her time to shine and I choose to believe that once I unleash her my life is going to change for the better. See how we form new beliefs around our success and our goals? Now keep in mind, you can also write, "I believe..." without the "choose to..." however, don't progress to this unless it is TRULY one of your beliefs.

It is necessary to only recognize blocks that are there and not create new blocks or potential blocks. If you don't have a specific belief holding you back don't make one up. If you believe nothing is holding you back then you are self-sabotaging because if nothing was truly holding you back you would have everything you want in life. So BE CLEAR and HONEST!

The best part about this is, when you recognize and acknowledge, you then get to choose to release them by forming YOUR own PERSONAL beliefs.

Go for it.... What do you believe about fully stepping into your most badass, best self and what do you now choose to believe?

_____

_____

_____

_____

_____

_____

_____

_____

_____

_____

_____

_____

_____

_____

_____

_____

_____

_____

_____

_____

_____

_____

OPERATION BADASS:

GAME PLAN

It's time to make a plan. It is necessary to take action and it is extremely helpful when we have an action plan. So, now is the time to get clear on the steps and the time frame that you are committed to in order to achieve your goals and own it.

I know, goal setting to some of you may seem boring, but let's choose to believe differently, because this badass game plan is not going to be boring. Attach emotion from the outcome of achieving these goals to actually pursuing them.

We are going to begin by learning how to set goals and write them into existence so our identity can act from a space of them already being completed. It is important to create a short-term plan, midterm, and long term. Having this vision moving forward helps us to take steps in the right direction every day. Now I am not saying you have to plan out every moment of your life from going to the bathroom to the finger you use to turn on a light; we just need to take your big picture vision of your most badass self and make it more doable and achievable over the course of today to tomorrow to the next few months and so on. Eventually it just becomes you and you become it and that's that and then we can uplevel from there.

So, let's focus on creating a master plan. We want to be very smart about this while also being very big vision oriented. Don't underestimate your abilities, you are going to shift into this badass version of yourself quickly so consider the speed of which this developing badass performs. Similarly though, we don't want to self-sabotage by setting goals that are extreme and unattainable. Even though I believe we are capable of more than we believe and we are capable of so many things and can live a life without limits, it is important to set goals which are not only achievable but which feel right in our minds.

It all comes back to alignment and belief. If you set this HUGE goal and you feel disconnected from it and think it isn't possible and it scares you WAY too much, then you will NEVER hit it. Remember, we want to feel aligned with our goals, so set a goal which pushes you out of your comfort zone everyday but not goals which you don't have any belief in achieving in said time frame. Lifetime goals are awesome; however, we are going to take a year goal and break it down so the year goal is perceived much easier and your mind feels way better about reaching it.

Imagine as a child, your goal is to ride a bike on your own and know how to do it without any help. SO, you set this goal but it gets broken down into very attainable much less scary chunks. Normally starting with training wheels, then working your way up. Totally doable and progressive and even though it pushes you as a child it is something you know you will accomplish with these steps.

www.celestial.fit

Time to get to work on your game plan. If you need any reminders on how much you actually deserve to step into this, go back and read all your prior journal entries and revisit and perform them daily.

COMMENCING OPERATION BADASS!

OPERATION BADASS: GAME PLAN

PART 1: GOALS BECOMING REALITY

What if I told you, you could literally write your goals into existence? What if you fully believed and embraced this concept and made it your truth? And what if you did it? Well, we are about to. It is important that when we focus on our goals, we connect with them from a place as though they are already done. If we are always saying 'will' we are just going to keep putting it off until it 'is right' or 'it comes'. Why not start believing and acting as though you have already achieved your goals?

At this point I want you to dive deep into what becoming this most badass best version of you looks like over specific periods of time. When you are writing these goals out, write them as though they are done, and address what it means for you going forward, your life and then your next level. When we can highlight a level above our 'ideal' or our current goal then our mind sees so much more ability to actually achieve this first goal.

Here's what I want you to include in this badass game plan; who are you, what do you do every day, what do you eat, how do you act, who do you hangout with, where do you spend most of your time, what drives you, what do you do for a living, are you working, how much freedom do you have, what do you look like physically, what do you normally feel like, what are you doing more of, less of, what do you see every day, what do your plans looks like, what is your daily routine, what type of clothing are you wearing, shoes, what type of products do you use, what do you think about, what do you focus on, what do you talk about, and on, and on, and on.

GET SPECIFIC!

The reason why we need to be so specific is because we cannot hit a target that we cannot see. So, if you 'want to be fit' what does that LOOK like, FEEL like, and DO for you daily? Saying 'I am fit' is not enough. Elaborate. Maybe you consider the home you are living in, how many bedrooms does it have, what are the sizes of the beds, what food is in your cabinet and fridge? JUST DREAM!

Now, with these goals, we need to be real with ourselves as mentioned on the previous page. So, I recommend starting with your 12-month big vision picture to becoming more badass then breaking it down from there into increments; 12 months, 9 months, 6 months, 3 months, this month, this week, daily ☺.

From now on, every week, and every day you can choose to set non-negotiables and tasks which will get you closer to your ideal reality and self. So, if part of being more badass means getting healthier and reducing stress, then consider hiring someone to help you. If part of being more badass means joining a new class or club or sport, then maybe your first step is to research or ask around. Breaking it down helps us to really make our big vision dreams seem so much clearer and doable and much less overwhelming. If you experience resistance around this activity, especially the biggest picture, go back and review previous pages, remind yourself of your why's, connect to that emotion of if you DON'T do this for yourself what it means for you and your life moving forward, and then go for it, you got this!

Time to get to it! Here is an example: "I am so happy and grateful to have low blood pressure after hiring a coach, consulting with my doctor, and eating healthier and working out properly. Now that I have lower blood pressure my goal for next month is to focus on getting even stronger. Having low blood pressure has given me more freedom with my family, relationships, and day to day life. I feel so much more alive and available to live life to the fullest. I am such a badass. I am so ready to train for that hike up the volcano!" Always write as though it is done, "I am so happy and grateful to be such a badass accomplishing x, y, z, every day and feeling x, y, z and knowing I am x, y, z, and just frikkin' killin' it. With all of this, I am now able to x, y, z and it has allowed me to x, y, z."

Month 12

OPERATION BADASS: GAME PLAN

PART 2: BREAK IT DOWN

EPIC! Way to go! Now that you have your BIG PICTURE complete, now it is time to break it down.

Give time to think about the ways you can start achieving this grand vision. We are going to start chipping away at it chunk by chunk.

Overwhelm=sabotage= NO GOOD.

Take some time to rest or break or self-care and relax if you feel like you just unleashed A LOT of dreams and visions and now PLANS that you have not ever yet given the time they needed to. Be proud of the fact that you just allowed yourself to FEEL the emotion and identity of the better, more badass you!

Once you are ready, break it down over the next few pages, you are SO ready for this!

Month 9

Month 6

_____
_____
_____
_____
_____
_____
_____
_____
_____
_____
_____
_____
_____
_____
_____
_____
_____
_____
_____
_____
_____
_____
_____
_____

Month 3

_____

_____

_____

_____

_____

_____

_____

_____

_____

_____

_____

_____

_____

_____

_____

_____

_____

_____

_____

_____

_____

_____

Month 1

_____

_____

_____

_____

_____

_____

_____

_____

_____

_____

_____

_____

_____

_____

_____

_____

_____

_____

_____

_____

_____

_____

_____

_____

Weekly (each week place a new sheet of paper or new sticky note on top)

I like to make check boxes next to each one, too!

_____

_____

_____

_____

_____

_____

_____

_____

_____

_____

_____

_____

_____

_____

_____

_____

_____

_____

_____

_____

_____

Daily (each day place a new sheet of paper or new sticky note on top)

I like to make check boxes next to each one too!

_____

_____

_____

_____

_____

_____

_____

_____

_____

_____

_____

_____

_____

_____

_____

_____

_____

_____

OPERATION BADASS: THE UNLEASHING

YESS! I am soooo proud of you for taking the time to break it down into actionable steps, you should be proud too! This is really exciting and going to be a huge step in your journey. I am absolutely so excited to see you unleash your badass self, this is going to be epic!

In the unleashing process, we are going to look at the ways in which you can make this happen and be aligned with your action. Being aligned with your actions is going to make all the difference in the world. Action means nothing without any intention or feeling backing it. It is important to connect back to the emotional drivers which are leading you to actually set these goals in stone and make this massive plan and actually pursue it. When we can connect back to the emotion we can be reminded of our motivation and what gets us moving forward so we can actually achieve our goals.

If we act which is not in alignment with our end goal we find ourselves off track, running into some issues, fumbling and tripping along a bumpier road, and constantly having to reset or re-align. We don't want to have to constantly bring ourselves back to course. It is necessary to be aware of all of your actions and ask yourself, "Is this moving me closer to my goal or most badass and best self?" if the answer is no, then, DON'T DO IT! Focus on something that always aligns with your goal and keeps you on that path and journey towards betterment and badassery.

Unleashing your inner badass best self means committing to making it happen, to taking consistent action, and then of course to loving yourself throughout the process and as you make these breakthroughs. Considering how much you just did for yourself and your identity, you may already feel more badass than you did before, yay! Tap into that energy and feeling and let's crank it up!

It is so easy to write out our goals or our dreams or what we 'want'. In reality though, getting specific requires more work and some internal breakthroughs so we are about to bring even more of those out of you. I am sure you ran into some resistance or questioning the 'how' or even 'if' it could be done and let alone done by you! You need to begin stepping into this badass version of yourself; and I mean really stepping into this new you. It relates a lot to what I say about having the perfect body which is, "Having the perfect body won't make you love yourself, but loving yourself will make your body perfect" ☺ Agree? We must step into it NOW not 'when we have x' because if we wait we never actually take the steps necessary to get there!

This next section is going to ask you questions that will lead you to having more clarity and give you an even deeper understanding and vision on the things which you can start today to then branch into your badass self. We are really going to be tapping into the energy, the feeling, and the IDENTITY of this version of you.

www.celestial.fit

We know you love your current self and are working to up-level that love; so now we want to look at what the love is looking like as your badass self. It is just another key part of your journey as the more love we can give to ourselves the better!

GO, UNLEASH!

OPERATION BADASS: THE UNLEASHING

PART 1: MAKE IT HAPPEN, BADASS

This is where things get really fun, I mean, reeeaaalllly fun...

It is time for you to start making it happen. You have set your goals, you have narrowed down your big vision, and now it is time to make it all come to life, starting now, today, right this moment. Yep, how does that feel? Knowing you are about to totally make this badass version of you happen?

All right, so maybe you feel really good about your Badass game plan, and you should! But, believe it or not, we are going to take it a step further. There are more questions to be answered to allow you to fully step into this version of you right now. You know those goals people set and put off for years or never get around to actually achieving them because they never hit the ground running with them OR they never take it off the ground? Yeah, I am not going to let that happen to you!

So, in order to start making it happen we do need some more insight onto what we can do to make it happen. This is where cracking open and

UNLEASHING that badass within comes to play massively. There are 3 questions which I am going to ask you and I want you to ask yourself these questions at the start of everyday or if you are ever wondering what you should be doing to improve or unleash more badassery.

These questions are not meant to make you stress over the how or question if this is 'good enough'. Again, if you run into blocks, revisit your beliefs, your goals, and your intentions. Listen to yourself but also know what is serving you and what is not. Learn from emotions and experiences and move forward.

Come on now, let's bust out your badass, today and everyday this is a great thing to consider and ask yourself. So, let's do this.

What can you do to begin stepping into this badass version of you?

You can date these and add to it daily or create a nice big list of things you need to do and ask yourself daily!

(Refer to this and RE-brainstorm for the next question)

_____

_____

_____

_____

_____

_____

_____

_____

_____

_____

_____

_____

_____

_____

_____

_____

_____

Celeste Rains-Turk

What do you need to do today and in general to begin stepping into this badass version of you?

You can date these and add to it daily or create a nice big list of things you need to do and ask yourself daily!

(Consider what you need to think about, believe, take action on, release, let go of, give up, trust, etc. the whole 9!)

_____

_____

_____

_____

_____

_____

_____

_____

_____

_____

_____

_____

_____

_____

_____

_____

OPERATION BADASS: THE UNLEASHING

PART 2: ALIGNED ACTION

Let's look at alignment now. Since you have set action items for yourself and will be doing so daily if you choose to, it is important that these actions are aligned with your big vision. Sometimes we can be presented with other tasks or 'opportunities' or even people and things which do not serve us in pursuing our greater existence and our best selves.

When we consider the action we take, it is important to always beg the question, "Is this moving me closer to my identity/big vision reality?" When we find that the answer is no, we must choose a new task, when we find that the answer is yes we must pursue it and amplify its affect with proper intentions! There is no need to do anything, see anyone, pursue anything, have something, or think about things which do not further us on our path to growth and betterment.

Let's say you know a huge part of your badassery is being fit and healthy. If every day you chose to fill your body with junk food, or over eat, or under eat, would that be moving you forward in your path? NO! It's a big deal to stay in alignment with your big picture. If one does not stay clear in the pursuit of any goal or new reality, one is unable to actually own it and therefore, achieve it at the pace they desire or sometimes even at all.

I mentioned prior that we know when something is right, we know when something feels right, and we know when we are doing something which serves us in the long run. It should feel amazing, it should feel powerful, it should feel like growth. Sometimes growth can feel uncomfortable and raw, that is a great feeling because deep down you still know and recognize that it is accelerating your journey in achieving your goals. It should be a non-negotiable in your mind to only pursue the things which move you forward in your journey. Keep in mind, if you do anything which does not feel right, don't beat yourself up for it, recognize it, learn from it, and MOVE ON! No use in wasting time moping about it. Just release that, understand you can't go back, find the lesson, remember the lesson, reset intentions, and get your ass moving, kindly ☺

I am creating a diagram/drawing below to share the importance of staying in alignment. This should help to put things into perspective for you moving forward. Remember, the question is always about if what you are doing is aligned with the 'end' result/greater vision. (We all know there is no end, only up-leveling or regression; choose to up-level.)

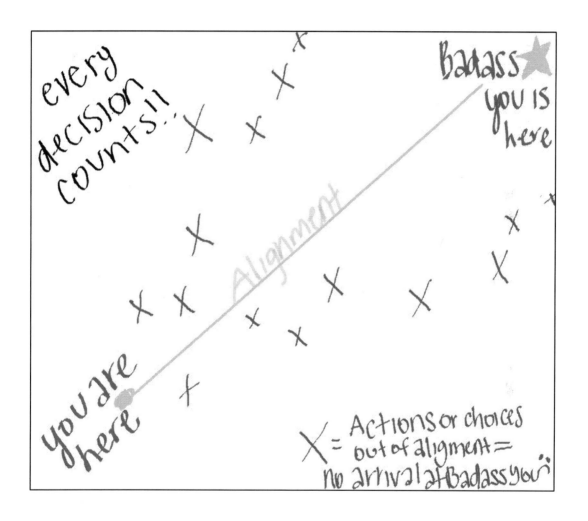

OPERATION BADASS: THE UNLEASHING

PART 3: LOVING YOUR BADASS SELF

Similar to the Operation Badass: Appreciation exercises, it is necessary to now note what it is you love about your Badass Best self. Keep in mind you do NOT have to wait until you are 100% this person. We are constantly and consistently growing so you are always going to find ways to progress and change overtime so it is important that you step into your best reality, what you really want to see yourself become, and acknowledge what you love about yourself as this person. This will give you even more reason to begin stepping into this identity every day. Since you love yourself and we like to feel loved and appreciated, it will be a great emotional driver and connection to your reasons, whys, and action taking. You wouldn't want to hate who you become so recognize now what it is you love about this version of you.

When taking the time to do this keep in mind you have limitless possibilities so forget about the "what ifs" or the "when I..." put more focus into the NOW rather than the HOW. You have made the decision that this is who you are and who you are becoming and growing as so it is necessary to appreciate this version of you. Consider all the ways this version of yourself speaks to and thinks about you. Is it uplifting, is it serving you, is it exciting, is it warm? What does it sound like? How do you show up in the world, how does the world see you (do you care-it's okay if you do just recognize what it is you care about them seeing you as and why)? What is your daily routine like, what are you eating, does this make you feel great? Remember, these are all ways you can show yourself love so think deep into what it is you do as this badass version of you showing yourself love daily. Do you pamper yourself, do you go out to eat, do you live in luxury, are you listening to your heart and what you want, do you embrace who you are every day?

Go deep, ask yourself questions. Know what it is that makes you TRULY love this badass version of you because you wouldn't want to become this version if it wasn't better, if it didn't make you feel better, if you weren't proud or feeling awesome about it. When we refer to ourselves in love we can generate even more love. Something I have learned is that there is nothing wrong with loving yourself but there is everything wrong with hating yourself. So step up to the plate and give yourself what you deserve. Thinking of this as a future tense scenario will not serve you or better you. Remember, this is NOW, this is happening, you have already decided, so give yourself some credit, how do you commit to loving yourself as this badass you?

Chances are you will find that this badass version of you has different ways of loving themselves so make sure you acknowledge that that is okay and normal because of course not just one part of us is growing, it is all of us. So, allow yourself to love differently too. I am 100% sure that the love you have been giving yourself and the ways you decided to uplevel your love is going to seriously shift since you are already growing into your better, more badass self.

Don't wait to love yourself, don't wait for the right time or when you have x, it is time to start right now, I guarantee you will be able to propel yourself closer to your ideal reality and big vision if you just allow yourself to have it right NOW and stop making yourself wait. You have no reason to hold back, this is the unleashing, you totally got this. Every time you make an excuse, have limiting beliefs, or give into 'norms' you are allowing yourself to be out of control and relinquish your power. This is about accepting your power and truly radiating it and unleashing it into the world. No one who ever got anywhere just stayed back, right? That wouldn't make any sense. Be aware of the way you treat yourself, think, and act as everything you do should be in alignment with your big vision and as that big picture grows so do you so everything must uplevel with that. Set this in motion, free yourself, let the massive force consume everything in its way-you are powerful.

Note what you love about your badass best self...

OPERATION BADASS: OWN IT

All right, badass, it's time to show yourself what you got. Once you show yourself, the world will notice, so just do you. When you are aligned, when you are taking the daily action when you are stepping into the identity daily, when you are tapping into that energy, when you are expressing love for yourself, there is only space to attract people, things, opportunities, and energy that you want to attract. When you decide to call this into your life, and you are this person, and you are totally owning your space, owning who you are, and owning your badass best self, there will be no more room for anything less than that. You will not achieve everything you want and desire unless you own it. You won't achieve your goals unless you become the person who achieves their goals. This is nothing but a choice to step into this better version of you daily. Know that you will never change today if you continue to be the person you were yesterday. It is necessary to be in this consistent state of the best version of yourself daily in order to grow. It is time to OWN IT.

When it comes to owning this, you need to apply everything. When you apply everything you also attract everything. When you don't apply anything you don't grow, so you don't change, and you just get worse. I have to be real with you, don't allow the time you have invested in yourself go to waste, this is the time where you fully embrace this kickass self.

You also need to be consistent. Anytime something comes up that could draw you back to old ways you must persist and you must endure. It is easy to hide, it is easy to stay in your zone of comfort, it is easy to stay the course of which you have followed for so long, it is easy to not give yourself what you actually want. But easy doesn't cut it. Badasses don't take the easy route, at least not in my world, badasses step up and step out, out of the comfort zone and into the zone of growth and making things happen. I don't know anyone who ever got where they wanted to be by staying where they are.

Walk the way your badass self walks, think like your badass self, talk like them, do things they would do, become that version of you. Because until you become that person, no space will be created for anything to come in that that person would call in. Own it means you OWN IT! If you could define what owning it would look like for you, what would that look like? What do you imagine, picture, see? What do you hear, understand, and take in? What do you feel, express, and relate to? What are you doing, what action are you taking, what is the energy like? KNOW it then OWN it.

The moment you decide to let things pull you away from the badass best you, is the moment you take steps backwards or off the path of alignment. When we continue to move forward with ease and a sense of lightness because we accept that we are polarizing, we are 'unusual', we 'have changed', we accept that not everyone is going to like us or love us or even hate us anymore. We accept that every person, thing, opportunity, etc., which leaves us is just a sign that room is being made for the best to come in. We accept that the fulfillment is coming, we accept that filtering is happening, we accept that this is the life we are not only deserving of but give ourselves permission to have as well. As soon as you give yourself permission and the okay to go through this, the easier it is going to feel, the easier it is going to be, the better your journey will be.

OPERATION BADASS: OWN IT

PART 1: APPLY

Application of your badassery is not meant to be left to one area of your life. It is meant to be applied to all areas of your life and propel your performance forward in all aspects. If we only focused on one area, everything else would fall short of amazing, and you deserve better than that. Not to mention every aspect of our life impacts the next. If our health is poor, but everything else is top notch, we are still at a loss. If our fitness routine is great but our mindset is not, the results will be hindered. It is necessary to place specific importance on all the areas of your life and ask yourself where you could improve. We are going to look at different areas of your life (not all but a LOT) which could be rated on a scale of 1-10 or however you rate things best to really see where your badass identity is going to need to spend more time.

Now, if there is no emotion, reason, or why behind improving each area of your life then there is no point. We have to back our action, or our thoughts around this with a why as we began with. It wouldn't serve you much to just see that your health needed to change. Actually committing to it, the outcome, and your reason for wanting it is what generates the best change. Of course, stepping into this identity is no joke. It is you, it is your desire, it is everything you want, it is exactly what you know you need to feel absolutely amazing, so we must make sure we always have this identity. The moment we put on an old mask, front, or identity we are actually stepping out of the identity which we are striving to completely fulfill and step into. So, when or if this happens, recognize it, see where it is coming from, ask yourself why, and then ask yourself what badass you would do, and apply, again, and again, and again.

What would it mean to you to carry this best version of yourself in all walks of life? What would it be like to totally, completely, utterly own this version of you without a doubt? What if being in this identity in multiple areas could aid in your feeling of complete alignment and fulfillment and wholeness? Now, can you pin point a time in your life where you have been totally crushing it in one or two areas of your life then feeling completely smashed and overwhelmed or behind in others? Maybe you feel that way a bit now? Either way, it is difficult to wrap our heads around this at times because we are dominating in one area, shouldn't we be dominating in every area? Here's the key though, if the energy for the identity is higher in particular aspects of your life it is most likely because the energy behind your reasoning is stronger there than in other areas. It is important to recognize this so in this next exercise when we think about why improving would benefit us, we can then go away in life and raise our energy in order to increase the vibration to receive more in all other areas.

Now we are going to start putting this application into action. The most important thing is to look at this through very honest, real, and open lenses as you have been throughout this guide. The deeper, more real you can get with yourself the better. I encourage you to go back to your beliefs and love for yourself before this to allow the fuel and energy to be from a place of sincere self-love rather than judgement. There is always going to be room for growth, improvement and upleveling so focus on the fact that all the answers to your next big breakthrough are literally within you right now, sometimes they just need a little pull out. Flow, trust, and reveal so you can own it further through application of the areas which need more love and attention for growth; let's do this!

Rate the following areas of your life then seek reasoning for improvements

Please Keep in mind these are not the ONLY areas of your life, you may discover more and want to add more. This is your time to be really expansive with this exercise. Some things may even stem from others, just flow with this process and take the time to assess your life and highlight where change is necessary for growth to occur.

LIFE PURPOSE:

_____

_____

_____

WHY IMPROVE?

_____

_____

_____

_____

_____

_____

_____

_____

CONTRIBUTION:

_____
_____
_____

WHY IMPROVE?

_____
_____
_____
_____
_____
_____
_____
_____
_____
_____
_____
_____
_____
_____
_____

RELATIONSHIPS:

_____

_____

_____

WHY IMPROVE?

_____

_____

_____

_____

_____

_____

_____

_____

_____

_____

_____

_____

_____

_____

_____

_____

FAMILY:

_____

_____

_____

WHY IMPROVE?

_____

_____

_____

_____

_____

_____

_____

_____

_____

_____

_____

_____

_____

_____

_____

_____

WEALTH/FINANCE:

_____

_____

_____

WHY IMPROVE?

_____

_____

_____

_____

_____

_____

_____

_____

_____

_____

_____

_____

_____

_____

FREEDOM:

_____

_____

_____

WHY IMPROVE?

_____

_____

_____

_____

_____

_____

_____

_____

_____

_____

_____

_____

_____

_____

_____

_____

_____

PASSIONS/ENJOYMENT:

_____

_____

_____

WHY IMPROVE?

_____

_____

_____

_____

_____

_____

_____

_____

_____

_____

_____

_____

_____

_____

_____

HEALTH:

_____

_____

_____

WHY IMPROVE?

_____

_____

_____

_____

_____

_____

_____

_____

_____

_____

_____

_____

_____

_____

MINDSET:

_____

_____

_____

WHY IMPROVE?

_____

_____

_____

_____

_____

_____

_____

_____

_____

_____

_____

_____

_____

_____

_____

WELLBEING:

_____
_____
_____

WHY IMPROVE?

_____
_____
_____
_____
_____
_____
_____
_____
_____
_____
_____
_____
_____
_____
_____
_____

OPERATION BADASS: OWN IT

PART 2: PERSIST AND ENDURE

Imagine if you could literally snap your fingers and be present in that identity instantaneously. That is what we want to be capable of daily to the point where it isn't an identity we have to step into, rather it is ours and now we are stepping into an even HIGHER identity. So, let's say one morning you revisited a lot of, if not all the activities from this book, and you stepped into the identity of a badass, and you are feeling really awesome and empowered, and then you step outside, get in your car, and then get cut off by a driver, and BAM you start being REACTIVE and you're no longer RESPONSIVE in the way your badass identity would be and you have just re-stepped into the old version of you. Doesn't feel great, does it?

Well, definitely not a productive decision to dwell on this. Instead just ask yourself what you could have done, should have done, and can do if it happens again. Learning from it will actually serve you, beating yourself up will not. The emotions are only there because the lesson is not yet there. So, choose to learn, daily, from a space of your higher identity, your best self, the you you seek to be NOW in order to become it without thought or question later.

Persisting and enduring means staying strong, staying true, and holding your own. Persist and endure means approaching and interacting in situations with a level head and clear identity. Persisting and enduring means you, your mind, and your actions are in true alignment even when the going gets tough. It means you never back down. Persisting and enduring comes from consistency in action and response. Persisting and enduring is a choice, like all things. We make decisions every day from the moment we wake up to the moment we go to sleep. It is no surprise that sometimes our decision-making times can be challenged by old beliefs, limiting thought patterns, and our subconscious mind. However, when we can step outside of that, and realign as we did throughout this book and get in touch with what the level we are committing to playing at is and what the identity we choose to 'settle' for is, then we can persist and endure knowing if anything happens, there is a lesson.

When we persist, it means we grow, we don't get lazy, or let things slip. It doesn't have to be hard, or difficult. There doesn't have to be struggle. You get to choose the ease of which you act, receive, believe and exist. When we endure, it means we have learned, we have addressed situations, beliefs, or old behaviors. When we endure, we are not allowing anything to get in our way because we keep moving no matter what. Emotions turn into lessons so every situation is no longer backed in fear, or hurt, or guilt, or anxiety, or even sadness. Now, we are backed by knowledge, decisions, skills, and clarity. We endure.

The last exercise of this book is to ask yourself one question and one question only; "How do (or can) I commit to persisting and enduring through life, loving, knowing, and owning my best most badass self so I can continuously grow in this identity and always believe my way to badass?"

This is about committing to yourself, committing to your goals and plans. Committing to what you have laid out for yourself, and committing to stepping up every day to own who you are and who you are becoming. Committing means actual action, committing means jumping before you are ready. Committing means actually pursuing the physical form of the answers you have given yourself throughout this book.

Savor this. Take this in. Embrace it. Step into it. Put it to action. You got this. Be Badass.

"How do I commit to persisting and enduring through life, loving, knowing, and owning my best most badass self so I can continuously grow in this identity and always believe my way to badass?"

_____
_____
_____
_____
_____
_____
_____
_____
_____
_____
_____
_____
_____
_____
_____
_____
_____

SUMMARY

Wow. You should be so proud of yourself for completing this interactive guide and implementing my coaching. I am so happy for you and I encourage you to review, revisit, and refocus on all of these aspects daily; after-all, what you focus on you find.

Every day should start with clarity and intentions with the knowledge that you literally get to define who you are and everything around you, always; just like you defined badass on your own terms, literally. Every day you should be evaluating who you are right then and there, because there is always space to grow when we create it. So, create the space for growth by owning and recognizing your present self, loving and acknowledging your present self, and choosing to show yourself more love. Every morning and throughout the day recognize what you do for yourself that makes you feel great, or what you can do, and then commit to do that before the end of the week. You should make yourself just as much as, if not more, of a priority than everyone and everything else in your life.

Here's the thing to remember about becoming the best version of yourself though, you are never done, there is always potential that needs to be unlocked.

www.celestial.fit

So, discover and release the next best version of yourself consistently, daily, always. We cannot become anyone or anything more if we continue to do the same things we have consistently done or have always known. We must step outside of our norm and create a new level, a new reality, a new pattern for ourselves.

Of course, you never should change who you are; this is your soul x 10 x 100 x 100…and the list goes on. Accept that you deserve more, accept that you can give yourself time to dig deeper, accept that you are able to find all the answers within you when you finally decide to look. Evaluate your beliefs and the programs running through your mind. If that little voice comes up in the back of your head, acknowledge, release, and choose new beliefs with a badass smile on your face that screams 'I so got this…'

Everyday should be focused on creating anew. Everyday should entail creating space for results and positivity. We must commit to the result we desire with the certainty that there are NO other options, it's all or nothing because you are all or nothing with yourself because that is your minimum standard, that is what you deserve, that is what your badass self has decided. No back up plan, no waiting, no 'when this…' of 'if that…'. It is right here and right now.

We cannot hit a target we cannot see so depict your ideal self, daily. Get crystal clear, so clear to the point where you can feel that energy, embrace it, and totally step into it at any given moment; anchor it. Ask yourself who you must become in order to achieve the results you desire? Tap into the energy of this person all throughout your day and check in with yourself that you are living and acting from this creative, higher space.

www.celestial.fit

Since this is so focused on beliefs and literally believing your way to badass, it is necessary and important to be very aware of the beliefs you need to release, the beliefs you need to take on, the beliefs you currently have, and the beliefs your badass self would have on repeat. We must recognize our blocks in order to change for the better and we must be humble enough to know that if we are not where we want to be, if we are not yet at our ultimate identity, if we don't have everything we have set out to achieve then something is holding us back, whether we like it or not, we must recognize and release these blocks and limits so we can actually achieve and receive. Best part? Once you recognize and release, you also get to choose new beliefs. Again, everything is a choice, your choice.

Don't forget, you need a game plan, action is necessary for anything to manifest into reality. Yes, you have your big vision, but what's next, what goals do you have for the next 12 months, 9 months, 6 months, 3 months, 1 month, this week, today? Write them into existence and commit to action with your higher self in mind by asking yourself what action do you need to take in order to propel yourself forward into your higher identity. We must be specific, we must have our why, and we must set non-negotiables and take action on them to experience our growth in a positive direction and we must always act from the identity of our higher self so we can receive what the higher version of us receives.

Then, the unleashing begins, make this happen with aligned action, stay on your path of alignment and avoid straying. If straying occurs, don't dwell, just learn. Learning is what releases the emotion from the situation and allows us to truly move on and move forward so we don't get stuck or wrapped up in whatever action it was that wasn't really in alignment for us. Unleashing your inner badass self means you are committed to making it happen with consistent action and the power to jump. As I mentioned, the people who jump 'before they are ready' are the ones who hit the ground running first. Make the decision to jump. Ask yourself what you can do overall, then ask yourself what you can do today. Then commit to doing it and set these action items for yourself every day.

Of course, loving yourself is key. Get in touch with what you love about your most badass self. You don't have to wait to start loving yourself. There are always going to be ways to progress and grow so step into your higher identities and recognize what you love about yourself not only because you deserve to feel that love, but because it will give you more motivation and reason to step further into this identity and take action which gets you there. It is so necessary to appreciate who you are and who you are growing into, spend more time focusing on the NOW than the HOW and just embrace yourself and your growth and your journey. Never relinquish your power to limiting beliefs, excuses, or 'norms'.

Now it is time to own it. Go all in, call this into your life, decide that this is who you are, you own your space, you own your badass best self, and you have no space for anything less than that. You become the person who achieves the goals which you desire. It's about you making the choice to step into this better version of yourself daily, making the choice to apply everything, making the choice to attract everything you desire, and making the choice to grow. Don't allow the time and energy you have invested in yourself go to waste.

www.celestial.fit

Apply this badassery to all areas of your life. Recognize where growth and balance needs to occur and make shifts to get yourself there. Until you make the decision to become the best, most badass version of yourself, you will never have the space to actually receive all of the amazing growth, opportunities, results, and emotions that come with it. Stay strong, stay true, and hold your own with persistence and endurance in any and all aspects of life. Choose ease, choose flow, and choose certainty. Stay consistent in your identity; walk your badass walk, think your badass thoughts, talk your badass talk, and do the badass things you need to do.

This is the time where you either grow or you die. Literally, every day you choose growth or death and understand that there is no middle ground, there is no staying the same, you either progress or you regress. Either way it is your choice. What do you choose?

MOVING FORWARD

MOVING FORWARD

I first want to say that I am so glad you found my coaching to be beneficial in your Believe your way to Badass journey and redefining your beliefs, developing your self-love, and manifesting your way to your best, most badass self. As we both know, there is always room for growth, there is always a next level, you are always going to be aiming for more and reaching new heights. When you commit to yourself, to action, to learning, to development, and to growth, there is no way your growth won't occur.

I know you are the type of person who makes things happen, who takes action, and who owns who they are, loves who they are, and commits to being in a higher identity with certainty that they are receiving everything they want and desire and it is all happening right now. If you know that you are all of those things, and you know this workbook has helped you, and you know it will continue to help and impact you for the rest of your life, and you know you are ready for even more growth, then keep reading.

I would love to hear from you if you are interested in continuing to work with me. There are several ways we can work together, including 1:1 mentoring.

www.celestial.fit

So if you feel called to work with me personally whether it be mindset coaching for you, your life, your business, your health, your wellbeing, your confidence, or any other area of your life then please reach out to me via my website, www.celestial.fit or contact me via email or social media as I do only work with a select few individuals per month to ensure maximum value, commitment, and energy on all ends.

I do want to invite you into my VIP Building More than just a Body Membership Site and Global tribe of badasses. (www.celesterainsturk.com) Building More than Just a Body is all about improving your life, mindset, health, behavior, habits, confidence, wellbeing, fitness, nutrition, self-love, and of course, overall badassery.

With over $50,000 worth of coaching and mentoring each year, you can watch trainings, request specific coaching topics, download notes, and even ask me your own questions in our private Facebook tribe from anywhere in the world for much less!

Inclusive of Step-by-Step Coaching with Nutritional Guidance and Planning tools, Monthly Training Programs with specific coaching on how to make the program work best for you based on your goals, Mindset, Confidence, and Long Term Success Building, Wellness Coaching, Behavior Modification Planning, and so much more!

Learn how to Sustain Your Life- And Your Results and Watch your results dramatically compound as you apply your coaching every week! You will receive new strategies, new tools and action steps, a rewired mindset around fitness, a renewed love for yourself and the journey, and a revamped level of confidence, Aesthetic results matched by your confidence, wellbeing, new found mindset, and total shift around your journey to Building More than Just a Body, the real solution to a healthy, happy, painless, sustainable, long term journey.

Why spend years and years, and thousands of dollars that I've spent to get results, when you can just have access to everything I have learned, everything I have mastered, everything I have developed, and continue to develop, to receive ultimate success in fitness, health, lifestyle, wellness, and of course inner strength, mindset practices, and total confidence?

Here are *just a few* examples of what you'll learn:

- ✓ How to Set Goals and Actually Achieve them
- ✓ How to Train, Eat, and Think for any Result/Goal that you Have
- ✓ Developing your Daily Success Ritual
- ✓ How to Respond to Situational Eating
- ✓ Untapped fitness, nutrition, and result hacks
- ✓ Learn how to connect your mind to the muscle
- ✓ How to Focus on What You want to Find
- ✓ Remove Negative Self-Talk and Low Self-Esteem
- ✓ 7 Dimensions of Wellness and how to Develop Your Wellbeing
- ✓ How to Make a healthy, fit lifestyle fit YOU
- ✓ Step by Step Action Plans for Behavior Modification

This is perfect for anyone to start, improve, or up-level your fitness, life, health, wellness, behavior, mindset and confidence no matter where you are right now! I am committed to your success. My mission to help others achieve long term results by emphasizing the importance of mindset, self-love, self-confidence, and self-esteem building strategies alongside the proper training and nutrition regimen is something I want anyone to be able to have access to. I truly believe that fitness is about Building More than Just a Body.

This training is a gift. With people who are paying over $50,000 a year to access this training, it is unheard of to access this quality of impactful training for such a small investment. All I ask for in return is to please apply it. Follow the training every week, get to work on it, apply it, master it. Then go out there and use your results with your compounding success to create the body you love at the level you personally take pride in.

Plus, there are great bonuses:

FREE Access to apply for your own coaching topics to be answered in one of the weekly trainings,

FREE Access to Facebook Support Group. Jump into Building More than Just a Body VIP on Facebook and all of your questions answered so you'll never be left wondering "How do I...",

FREE Weekly notes to support the weekly trainings with Key points and resources at your fingertips, so you can take notes as you go.

www.celestial.fit

Remember there is no other Coaching Program in the WORLD where you can work with a key industry expert with this level of information every week for this small investment.

For more information and to join please head over to www.celesterainsturk.com.

If you have any questions, comments, or inquiries about working with me you are more than welcome to contact me via Facebook or email (celeste.rainsturk@gmail.com), and I would be happy to help you!

JOIN NOW! www.celesterainsturk.com

MISSION & TESTIMONIALS

I am on a mission to help others achieve long term results by emphasizing the importance of mindset, self-love, self-confidence, and self-esteem building strategies alongside the proper training and nutrition regimen. I truly believe that fitness is about Building More than Just a Body. I believe we can literally be, achieve, and have anything we desire in life with the proper focus and mindset, and everyone deserves to embody and radiate confidence in who they truly are. I know that It's all about emphasizing placing immense love, respect, value, and worth on yourself every day in your journey of consistent and constant up-leveling

Notes from those who I have impacted with the Building More than Just a Body Movement... ☺

"My name is Alexis and I've been working with Celeste for a month and in that month I have seen so many changes in my body that I didn't think we're even possible. I have gained so much self-confidence and self-love from this program which I never imagined possible. I now know my personal worth and can see my growth. Using this program has made it so easy to understand what it is I need to do in order for my body to achieve the goals I want it to. From the food plans to the workouts and all of the motivational videos I have never been more motivated to get into the gym every day and create a

stronger happier me! I could never thank Celeste enough for all she has encouraged me to do!" -Alexis H., Southern California

"I didn't realize how incredible this program is. Everyone needs to be invested in something like this. I'M TELLING THE WORLD. I am so excited, I just watched the first videos and I am doing the self-worth activity and I am already crying because I haven't felt this good in months. I AM WORTH IT, I am so glad I finally decided to invest in myself and my happiness." -Suzie S., Southern California

"I had an amazing opportunity to work with Celeste one on one. Throughout our sessions she taught me various moves to tone my upper and lower body. She was very knowledgeable when it came to working specific muscle groups with me. She was even more amazing when it came to the discussions of nutrition and how it goes along with exercise to build healthy habits.

Subsequently I went on to purchase a lower body toning program from Celeste. It was a series of ever changing routines to target glutes and legs. I immediately saw results which by far exceeded my expectations!

On top of all of this, Celeste provided unconditional moral support and expertise in calorie intake and a healthy diet. But the most important thing I had learned in the process was that building a healthy body begins from within. I learned self-love and self-acceptance! After all, it was so much more than building just a body!" -Elena N., Southern California

"*Love your real raw passion for creating a more positive balanced life for people whom you connect with. I love how young, passionate and driven you are which has and continues to inspire me each day, so glad we connected!*" - Katie M. Melbourne, Australia

"*I feel amazing physically, mentally, emotionally, and all that jazz. If me from four months ago saw me now, she wouldn't recognize this happy, skinny, beautiful person. I have so much more confidence in general and I'm really super glad I decided to enroll in your program.*" –Brooklyn, Southern California

"*Thank you for setting up a plan for me this year. So far in the past couple months I dropped 30 pounds, 3% body fat, and my vertical jump went from 29 to 35 inches. The plan you made fit really well with what I have been looking to achieve.*" -Matt H., Southern California

"*Right from the beginning Celeste made me feel like I belonged and her soul purpose was to help, support, coach and encourage me, even though she had other clients as well. I don't know how she does it, but she gets deep into your soul to help you release what is holding you back from being your absolute best self to build more than just a body! She is so compassionate, understanding and gives her whole heart to help you. Thank you so much Celeste! You have made such an impact on my life already.*"-Sonia M. South Australia

"Celeste Rains-Turk is one extraordinary young lady. Her love that she has to help another human being amazes me because it comes deep within her soul. Celeste has inspired me beyond belief with her knowledge and wisdom and I have learned so much from her because she believes in fully of what she teaches and that belief is that we are all worthy and we all matter. She does not take her uniqueness for granted and she uses her personal gifts and skills to bring the best out in us. Celeste is one woman that is making a mark in this world and she has only hit the tip of the iceberg. Amazing is not a strong enough word for this young lady. Thank you for all that you do and continue on changing the world with one life at a time. You rock!" –Pat Pilla, New York

"How my life has evolved since working with Celeste where do I start I come into this off a recommendation from my coach and I was like what have I got to lose I went in there just chasing a workout program and come out with a bible of knowledge she's not one to say it's ok it will be all good that's thing I love about her the most is she hits you with the truth at first you're like who are you then once you drop your ego you can tell Celeste is 100% right I'm grateful for the time and effort this superwoman puts into me I come from a place of less fortune due to my past but under Celeste the horizon just became clear. " -Nathan Coden, Queensland, Australia

"Just a quick thank you to you Celeste Rains-Turk for all your wisdom and inspiring words, to Erin for inviting me and everyone on this journey with me of self-love. I am in a bikini at wet n wild with my kids and I don't care. I'm at a place of peace with my outside as I am able to love myself imperfections and all" -Zara M. Sydney, Australia

www.celestial.fit

"Celeste is one of the most powerful young leaders I know. She has this unique ability to help people achieve rapid results, far beyond what they even initially think is possible. Her personality, enthusiasm for life and heart really set her apart from anyone else in her field. The results that Celeste has achieved at such a young age are outstanding and are a true testament to her incredible work ethic and her massive vision. Thank you Celeste for everything you do in this world and everything you are!" -Regan Hillyer, my personal mindset mentor and also kick ass client, Location Free

"Working with you was one of the best decisions of my life! If I didn't go for it, I wouldn't be as happy as I am. I have never been this happy about my body and I have learned to love myself for who I am! Because of you, I wouldn't have had the motivation to keep working out for as long as I have been." -Sara L., Southern California

"Celeste Rains-Turk has rocked and inspired my world. I have been working on self-esteem, nutrition, and working out since I was in grade school. I am 62 years old. IN your fb posts she shows knowledge and wisdom beyond her years. She is inspiring and motivational and nails topics all the time. Thank you Celeste!" –Beverly C., Southern California.

"I don't know how to describe it, I just feel cleaner inside, I know that sounds weird but it's just cleaner you know? I am not getting sick as often or feeling stomach aches, I just feel better" -Ricky C., Southern California

www.celestial.fit

"I hit the 20-pound mark today! I am now 20 pounds lighter than I was in January! This was my mini goal for the last few weeks to hit the 20-pound mark!"-Vanessa H., Southern California

"Celeste is a very gifted and highly evolved soul. She observes her thoughts and actions which allows her to move through life independently from harmful mental programs. I have watched her duplicate this amazing asset onto others and have seen her teach others to live as their highest self. Celeste is an amazing human being!" -Kyoshi Christopher DePalma, 7th Degree JuJitsu Black Belt, Southern California

"Celeste Rains-Turk is hands down one of the absolute best, most genuine, hard-working, and rare person you will ever come across in your life. Her mission is to help others in the best way she can with the best of her ability. She is completely dedicated to each and every one of her clients and seeks to experience their life fitness journey with them, whether they are located ten minutes away or another continent away. Celeste did not start her business to make money, she started it to promote and help people obtain a healthy lifestyle. It is rare to come across a trainer and life coach that is so dedicated to helping others the way she does. She truly has a beautiful soul and gives everything and everyone a hundred and ten percent of her effort. She genuinely empathizes with her clients and receives fulfillment out of the happiness of others. She has made a tremendous impact on not only my life, but everyone she meets. I am so lucky to call her one of my best friends". -Makayla J., Southern California

"Celeste is one of the most inspirational people in my life. Ever since I've met her, she's had a powerful impact on me. I've had the honor of coaching her with her online business for the past year and by getting to know her, I've come to realize that she is the embodiment of self-love. Celeste is a beacon for the world and has a balanced a life of fitness, mindset and serving others. She truly leads by example." -AJ Mihrzad Business Coach and Mentor, New York

"Working with celeste has been a life changing experience. I don't just say it, I truly mean it. The transformation I have gone through has been on so many levels. Spiritual, emotional and physical. I am feeling so much better in myself and I feel more confident and secure. I have realised that I am worthy of more. I am a beautiful, kind person who doesn't need to be validated by other people. Celeste asks all the right questions and made me look for the reasons behind my feelings and thoughts instead of focusing on trying to fix them straight out. It truly showed me how you have to look at the cause and address it before you can move on. I am in awe of the way she has made me realise things that no one has brought to my attention in all of my 25 years. Thank you for everything Celeste"-Zara Mulders. Sydney, Australia

"Grateful to Celeste Rains-Turk for doing this. The inspiration, the bringing like-minded people together, to support and encourage each other. THAT is what it's all about. We're on our own journeys, in our own lives, but connected...compassionate. LOVE THAT!" - Jeff S., Colorado Springs, Colorado

"Working with Celeste is such an amazing experience! She seriously has a gift for cutting through all of the garbage and getting straight to the heart of the issues I had surrounding body image! I'm so blessed to have her in my corner and to keep me on track!!" -Rebecca Y., Weatherford, Texas

"Celeste is absolutely awesome. She is a flood of positive energy in my news feed every day. I participated in a Facebook 7-day challenge and it was amazing. I value myself, build myself up, etc. and yet the quantity and quality of things I took away from this challenge are huge. I have made changes and with Celeste's support, there are many more to come. I love me! Thank you Celeste" -Amity C., Paris, France

"Working with you was such an amazing experience, you opened me up on the inside so I could actually realise what was holding me back. You were so open and friendly that I felt completely comfortable with you to be able to share my thoughts and feelings!

I really appreciated you coming into my life and am so grateful for the help you have given me! Xxx" -Rikki K., Wallaroo, South Australia

"At the beginning of my trek to becoming super fit I was pretty lost. Planning my food schedule and managing to make it to the gym was tough but thanks to Celeste I was able to get motivated. She developed my whole meal plan and even helped me with certain workouts to target certain muscles. I definitely appreciate what she has done for me, my whole lifestyle changed and even my body! Thanks for everything Celeste!" -Justin N., Southern California

www.celestial.fit

"*Celeste meal plans have helped me reach my goals into becoming stronger and gave me a different perspective on fitness. Without her I wouldn't be where I am today with my fitness level! Thank you Celeste for all you have done!!*"-Ricky C. Southern California

"*Celeste takes the meaning of unconditional love to a whole new level. As a coach, she has helped me break through deep, limiting beliefs in a matter of minutes.*

As both a coach and a friend, she will always have your best interest at heart, she will be rigorously honest with you, create a safe space for you, and show up for you 100% without fail, every single time.

She will kick your ass when you need it and have faith in you when you don't have faith in yourself. You will get the body you always wanted, but you will get so much more than that! Building More Than Just A Body isn't just a catchphrase with this coach. She actually walks the walk.

The fact that you're lucky enough to have come across this woman, means you owe it to yourself to get to know her better. She's an amazing person to have in your corner, and in your life."-Tara Daylami, Las Vegas, Nevada

"*I feel so great! I've never stuck to working out for this long and I'm so impressed by myself that I'm doing this! On top of that I can tell differences in my body and even though they aren't huge I am proud of myself that I'm doing this. And it's all thanks to you and I'm so grateful!!! P.S. These workouts are all different and fun and they are kicking my butt and I like it :)*" -Sara, Southern California

www.celestial.fit

"Celeste is a bright light in an often dim world. She has a strong sense of who she is and what life's about and I love that she lights the way for those who are unsure about what they want and what's possible. Sometimes I worry about the youth of today and what kind of future they will create, though Celeste's insights have revealed time and time again that she's wise beyond her years and that potential in her generation will not go to waste.

I really admire Celeste's dedication to growth & learning and absolutely love the passion that bubbles out of her when she speaks about ideas and concepts that excite her. She's been through a lot to get to where she is today and I'm always excited to see what she does next... I think big things are coming!" -Bianca Spears, Sydney, Australia

"Hey Celeste!! Thank you so much for our conversation the other day. I'd been needing a push to take a time out for myself just to re-align with myself, who I want to be, and how I want to show up in this world. You helped me focus in on the areas that I had been neglecting and get clear on the vision I have for myself. After talking, I looked a lot deeper into what we talked about, had conversations I'd been putting off, and felt a huge weight release from my shoulders as I felt like I connected back with the impact I want to make in the world. You asked the right questions to put me on the right track and help me open up to further self-discovery. You're a gift to this world, and I can't wait to see the magic as our journeys intersect more and more!" - Suzie M., Manchester, New Hampshire

"Thanks to Celeste and to everyone in this group for being living proof that there is still a lot of good in this world." -DeShauntel Lewis

"Celeste is an amazing trainer and fantastic person. She is dedicated to helping others achieve the best lifestyles they can and will help an encourage them every step of the way. As a trainer she has helped me move my life in a healthier, more active direction and as a person brings light to all those around her." -Cory Y, Southern California

"One of many things that really resonates with me about Celeste's mission is that she makes a BOLD stand in fitness being about Building More than Just a Body. I love her conviction and belief she pours into people to commit to a life full of healthy habits while emphasizing the importance of placing immense love, respect, value, and worth on yourself every day. There is more than one dimension to health and fitness and I admire the tenacity in which Celeste brings her message to the world. She is a total expert and authority in elevating her clients confidence in themselves. Congratulations on the release of your new book Celeste! Big love, Robyn x"- Robyn Nikora Scott Bali, Indonesia

"My weight has always been a "problem", always something I so badly wanted to change until it come to actually working hard at the gym, or when I was faced with a plateful of donuts. My life was a non-stop diet and exercise plan and I constantly felt like I was failing at. I heard about Celeste and I decided it was time to get help.

Right when I contacted Celeste I knew she was going to 1) change the way I felt about my body and 2) totally kick my butt into shape.

She immediately got me on a workout and eating plan that was perfect for me. It was no small commitment. I spend longer cooking and preparing my meals, and spent more time at the gym.

Celeste provided me with a workout plan, as well as a schedule in which we could meet with each other. We would work various body parts at different levels of difficulty. She trained me about 3 times a week and I cannot even begin to describe the changes I began to see.

Celeste coached me through my eating, exercise, and viewpoint on my body. She helped me push myself to reach incredible goals. I often woke up the next morning barley able to move but this motivated me more.

I not only could feel my results but I could see them. I strongly recommend Celeste's diet and exercise plans, but more so than this, her personal training."
-Suzie S., Southern California

"*First of all, I will start by saying that Celeste is one of the most genuine and down-to-earth individuals I have ever had the pleasure of encountering in my life. Sometimes, the instant you meet someone, you have no doubt that they will have a positive impact on your life no matter how significant. This is my experience of going from unhealthy and unhappy to loving all aspects of life and feeling and looking better than I ever have!*

Aside from playing sports and doing outdoor activities growing up, I did not start my fitness journey until senior year in high school. I had been going to the gym and "training consistently" for about a year at that point, but in reality was just going to the gym a few times a week, going through the motions, and eating like crap, and wondering why I wasn't getting anywhere. Starting senior year, I started doing a lot of research and trained meticulously making some significant improvements of about a 30lb increase but eventually hit a halt in progress and realized that not all of that 30lbs was muscle.

At that point, I decided that I was going to fully commit to the fitness lifestyle and I contacted Celeste about getting a custom meal plan to help me lean out as well as a proper training regimen to speed up the process. That was a major turning point in my journey and was undoubtedly one of the most important decisions I made along the road to success. It was a major transition for me as I was so used to eating anything and everything at all times having no clue at all or how to properly fuel my body. She helped me every step of the way whether it was showing me tips on how to prepare a certain meal or spice things up a bit to make it interesting and more enjoyable.

www.celestial.fit

Even to this day, years later we still keep in touch and share ideas and talk here and there despite our hectic schedules. She would even be there to answer any questions I had even if it was something personal, completely unrelated to diet and training which is what I believe sets her apart from the rest of the crowd. It certainly helped me get over a few mental hurdles and to stop setting limits for myself. Celeste has such a genuine passion for what she does and truly cares about the people she works with, which is something you cannot put a price on.

Looking back, I am so glad I went down this path. It has opened my eyes to a whole new way of viewing life itself, and her enthusiasm is what planted that seed that grew to be what is now all of the knowledge I have obtained since then by using the tools she gave me. I now eat 100% clean other than some cheat meals (pizza pizza pizza), and have taken the knowledge she has given me to be creative with eating on my own and I have never felt better. The passion for bettering myself and others can only improve from here on out. I am forever grateful for that.

On another note, at this point in time it was near the BEGINNING of her journey of teaching others and helping them reach their goals. It is incredible to see how much she has accomplished since then. Having a huge handful of clients, her extensive influence on social media, and especially WRITING THIS BOOK! It just goes to show how important this amazing journey is to her, and why she works so hard day in and day out to share the same experience with everyone else. Her story is unquestionably inspiring to me and I hope you think so too." -Josh Seiden, Southern California

www.celestial.fit

"*Celeste's Program is absolutely amazing. she has so many different workouts and exercises, you'll never find things repetitive or boring. This specialist tends to kick your ass and get you that body you really want!*

Celeste is there for you every step of the way, from the first step of designing an individualized food plan (for 1:1 VIP clients), to finally achieving results. She encourages you 100% and works with you constantly in order to make sure you get the best experience possible.

Despite any personal problems that arise in her life, Celeste continues to be amazing and supportive. If there is any problem with you finishing a workout, just mention it to Celeste and she will have altered your plan within the day.

Celeste's Program and Celeste herself is the best combination you could ask for. She is extremely passionate about everything fitness, which makes her the perfect trainer. Not only is she understanding and considerate of your individualized needs, she is highly motivating. She really wants you to succeed, and that makes all the difference.

Under Celeste's program, you WILL see results. it's impossible not to! They may not be immediate, but that's because Celeste does it the healthy way and in such and way that you will gain good habits for life. By following Celeste's plan, I have lost a ton of weight and am started to get that toned look. I look and feel amazing, all thanks to Celeste and my own motivations.

You would become hard pressed to find a better person to do what Celeste does This program is literally life changing. No matter how fat, thin, lean, swoll, short, tall, etc, a person is, Celeste will help them achieve their goals to

www.celestial.fit

her fullest extent. She's willing to help and go the distance, but it is up to the individual to really find the motivation to try. She can only help if you're willing to help yourself." -Brooklyn B., Southern California

To see more from those I have worked with, head over to my website.

www.celestial.fit

Work with Celeste

Join the VIP Building More than Just a Body Membership Site:

www.celesterainsturk.com

OR

See More Ways You Can Work with Celeste Here:

www.celestial.fit

ABOUT THE AUTHOR

Celeste Rains-Turk is a badass online fitness coach and mindset mentor changing lives every day by emphasizing fitness, health, wellness, behavior change modification planning, mindset, self-love, and self-confidence building strategies.

She is absolutely brilliant at making sure her clients gain confidence in themselves while providing them the tools necessary to continue their success day in and day out.

www.celestial.fit

She is a total authority on helping people achieve what they desire by instilling and acknowledging the importance of aligning the inner work with the physical results.

She believes that fitness is about Building More than Just a Body, we can literally be, achieve, and have anything we desire in life with the proper focus and mindset, and everyone deserves to embody and radiate confidence in who they truly are. She knows that It's all about emphasizing placing immense love, respect, value, and worth on yourself every day in your journey of consistent and constant up-leveling.

Get in touch with Celeste:

> Join her Free Tribe Building More than Just a Body: https://www.facebook.com/groups/buildingmorethanjustabody/
> Follow her on her Personal Facebook: https://www.facebook.com/TheRealCelestialFit
> Like her Public Figure Page: https://www.facebook.com/celestialfit/
> Follow her on Instagram: @celestial_fit https://www.instagram.com/celestial_fit/
> Watch and Subscribe to her YouTube: @celestial_fit https://www.youtube.com/channel/UC6WOMejsPSs07knjjj9L_rw
> Snap her on Snapchat: @celestialfit https://www.snapchat.com/add/celestialfit
> Pin with her on Pinterest: @celestialfit https://www.pinterest.com/celestialfit/
> Tweet her: @celestial_fit
> Linked in: https://www.linkedin.com/in/celestialfit

www.celestial.fit